Fantasy Coloring Book

Rosemary Scarborough

DEDICATION

There are too many people I need to thank for helping me along the way. From Caleb Simmons
For putting up with me while I worked drawing through the night;
to Amanda Reith and Monique Magee for preordering and reminding me that this is desired;
And my friends who put up with me skipping out on plans to ink pictures.

All of the images in this book are hand drawn and inked.
Please, let this help you get away from some of your troubles and be proud that you created something beautiful.
This was an amazing experience and I plan to create more coloring books.

Special thanks to Katherine Beam who did a collaborative image with me for this book
She did the lovely mermaid on page 6; the 3rd image. Also, Adam Donohue for writing the back text.

There are 25 images with page breaks so you have a blank page to plan colors and test technique.
Please feel free to use this as a tool to become a better artist!
If you are excited and would like to show me your coloring,
please tag Oracle Phlux on the social medias!

Thank you so much!

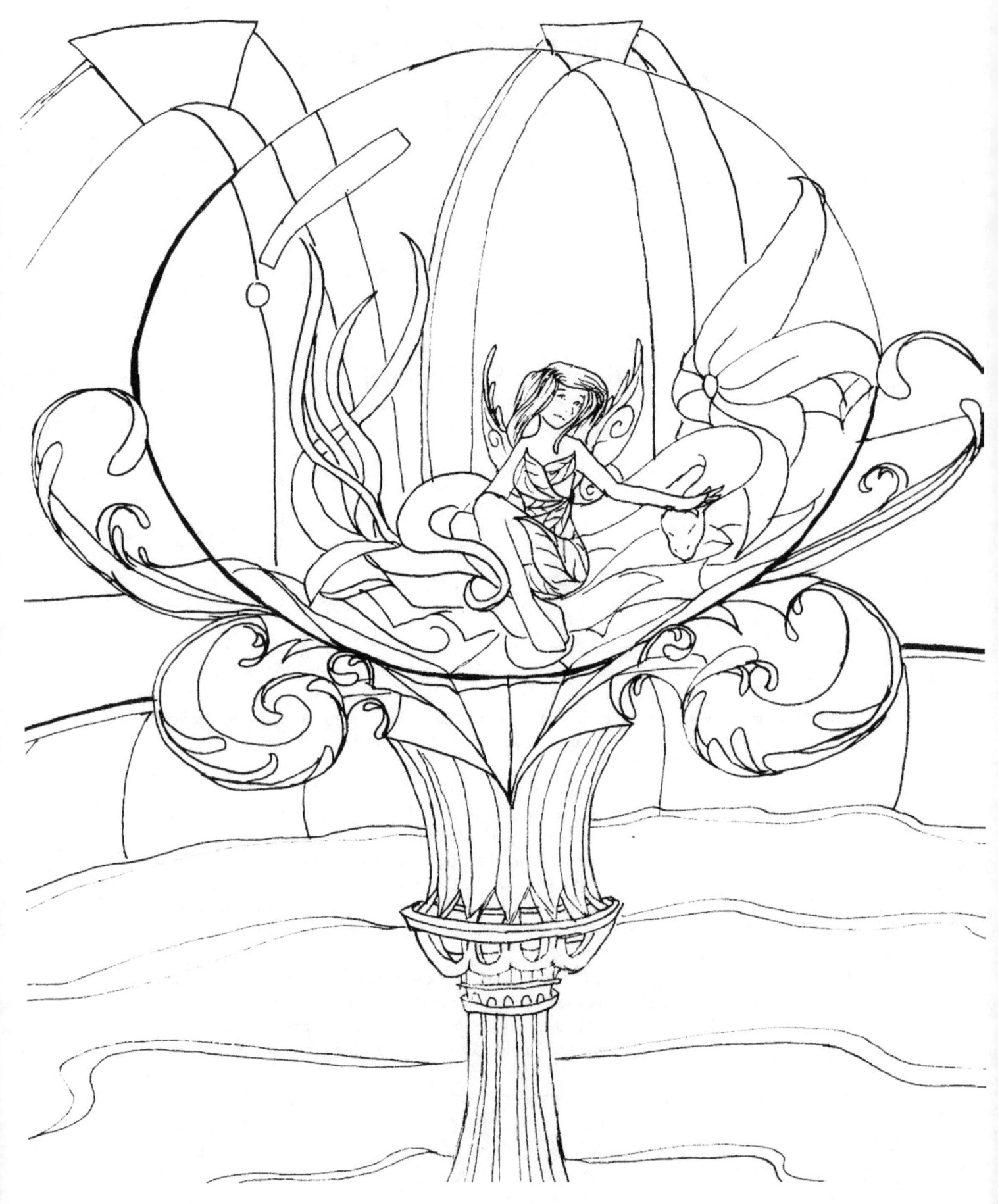

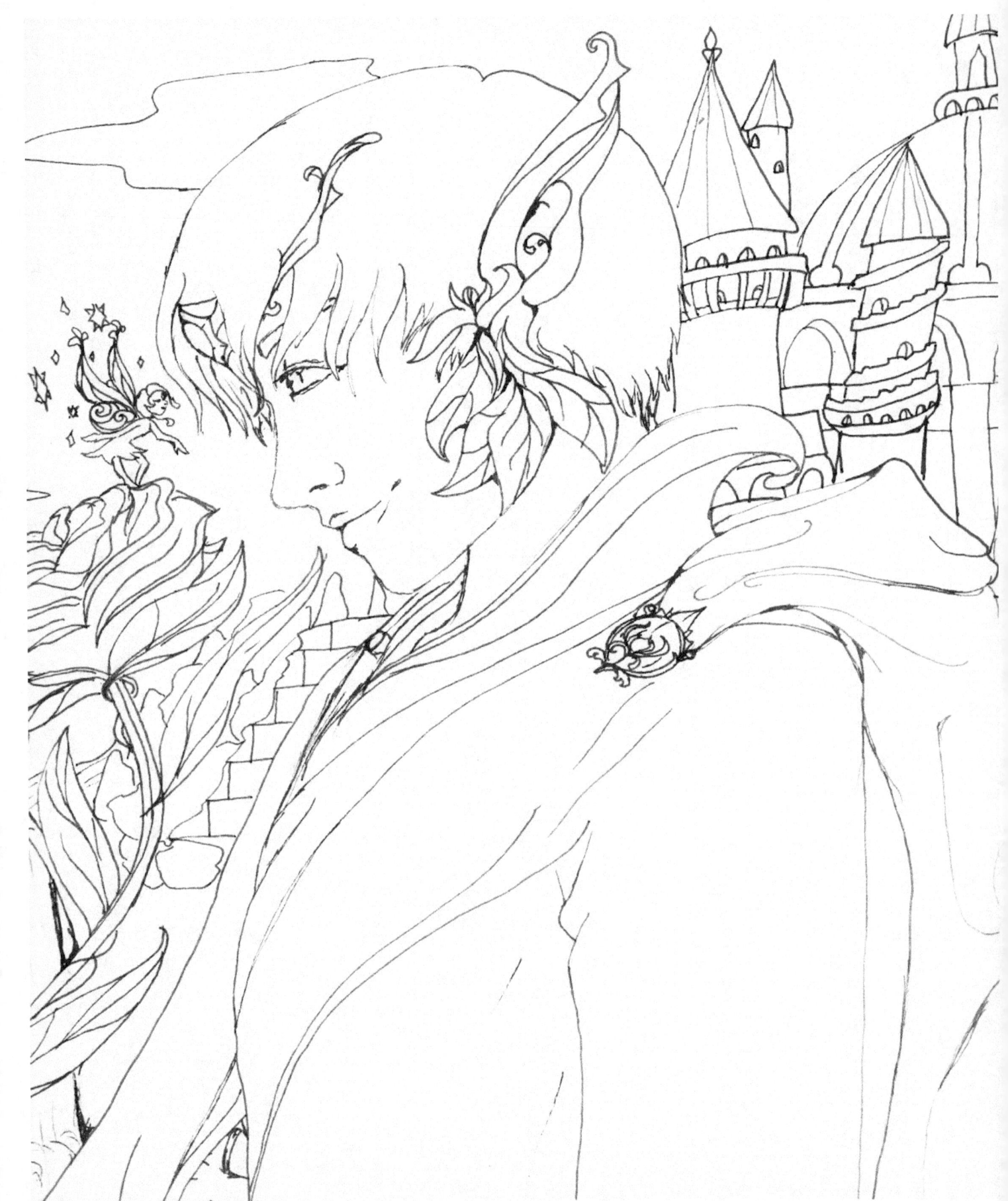

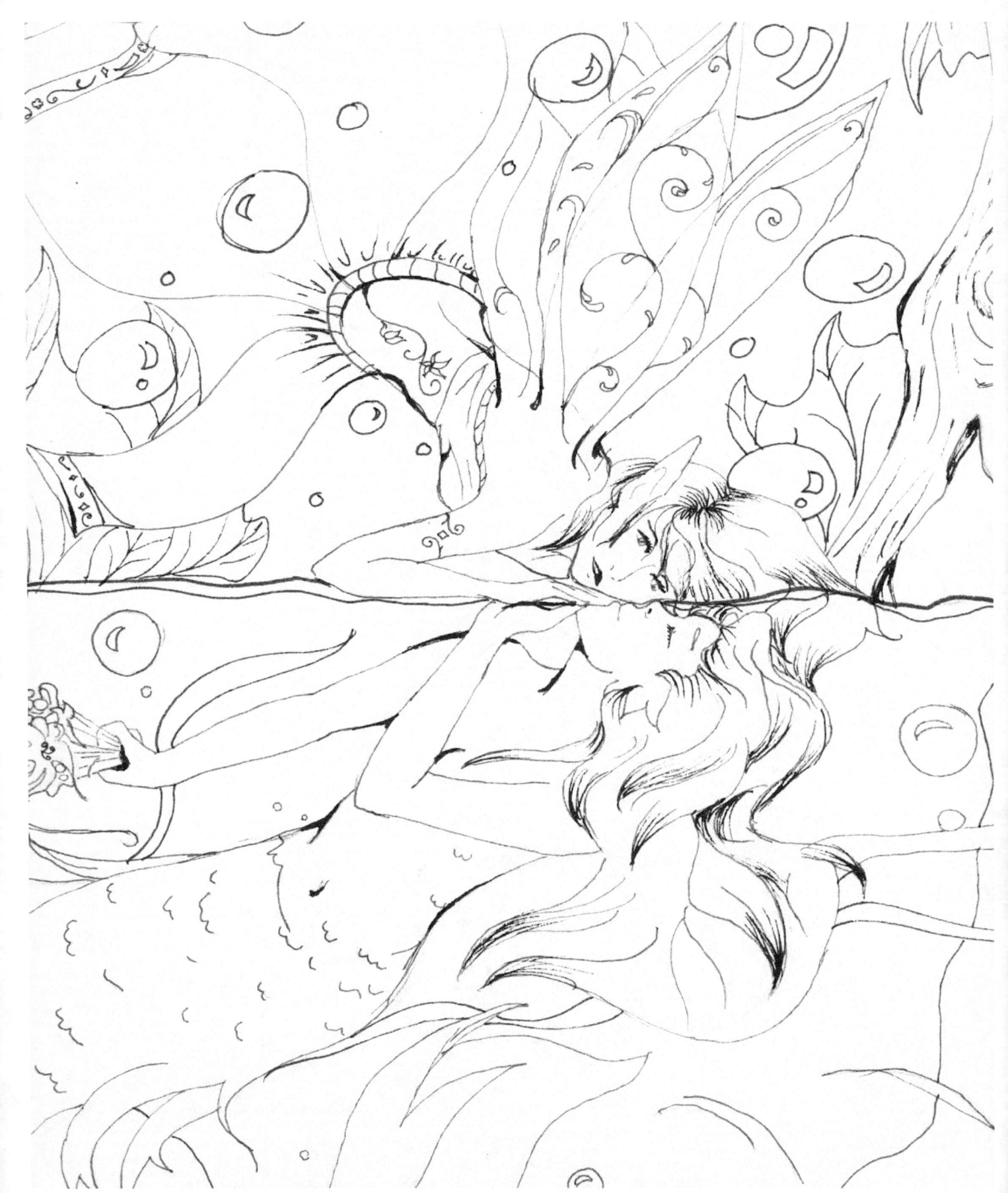

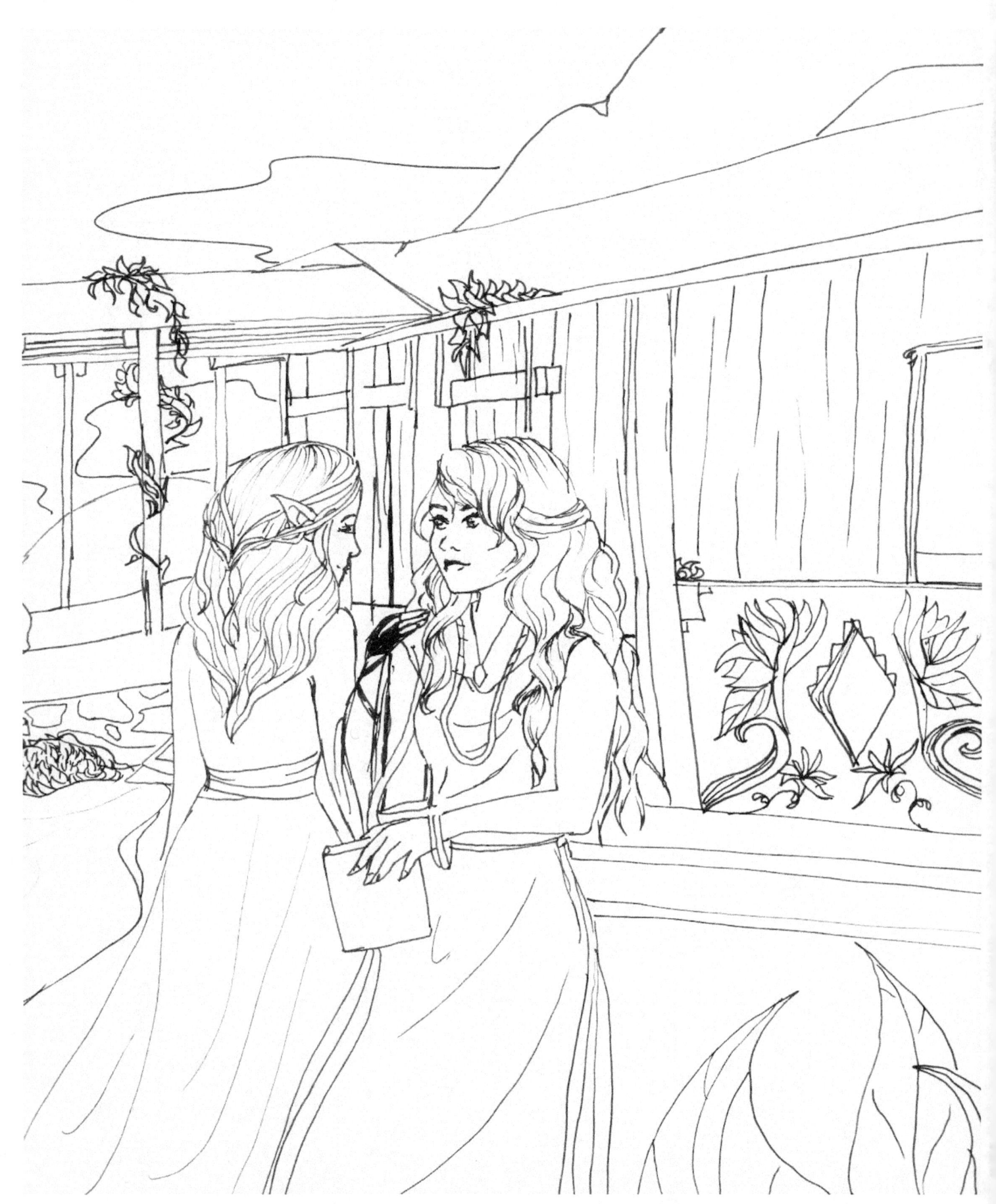

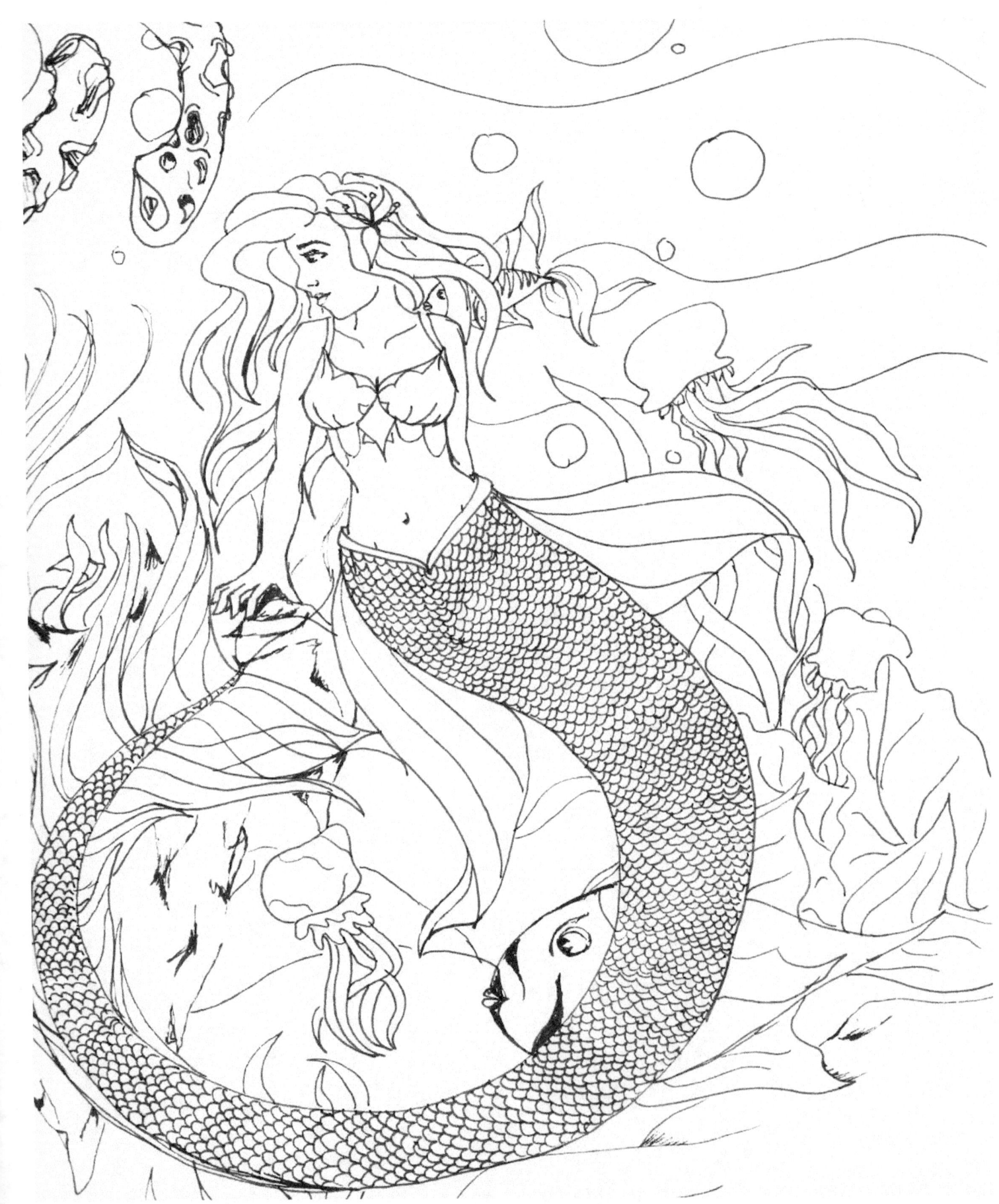

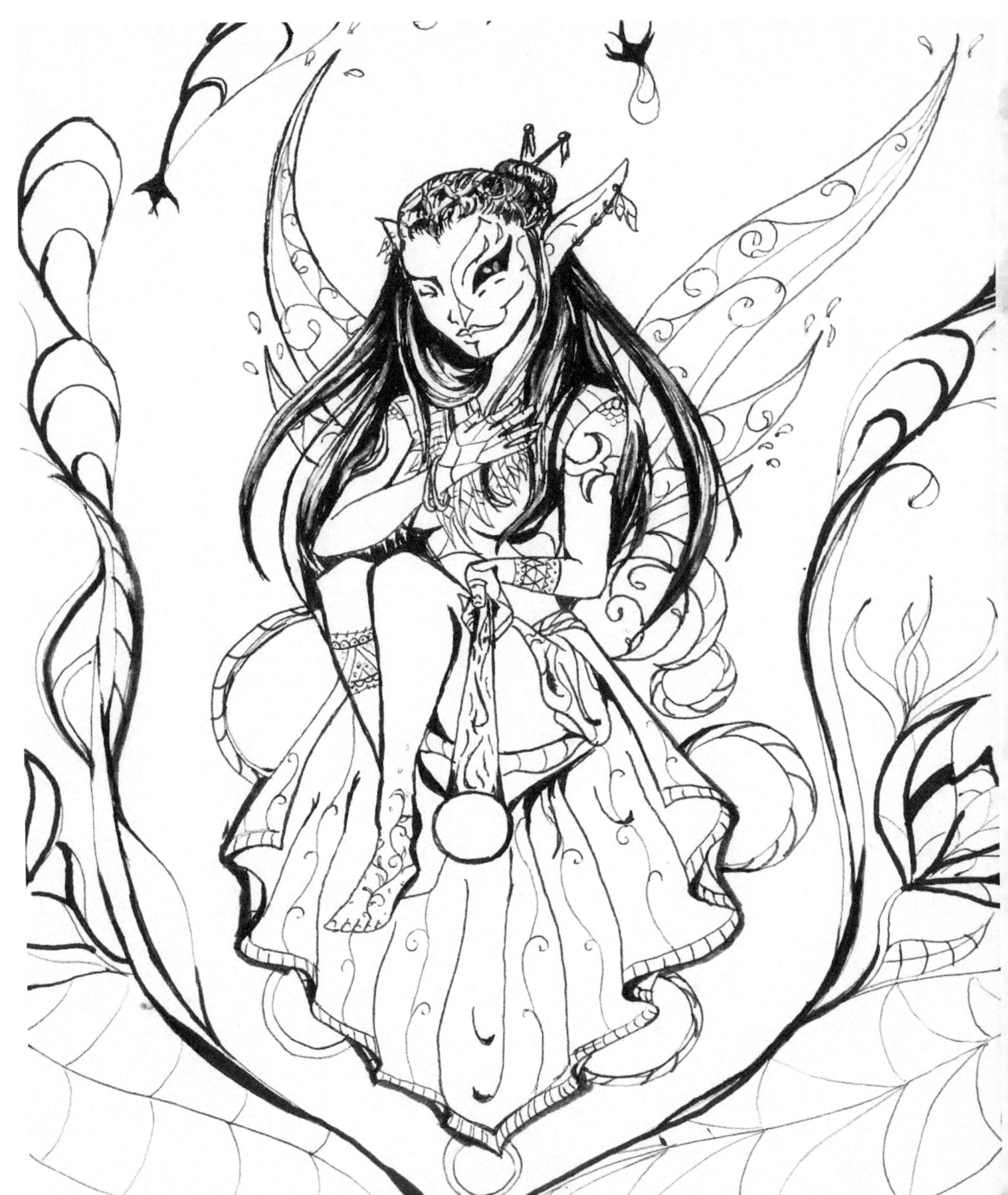

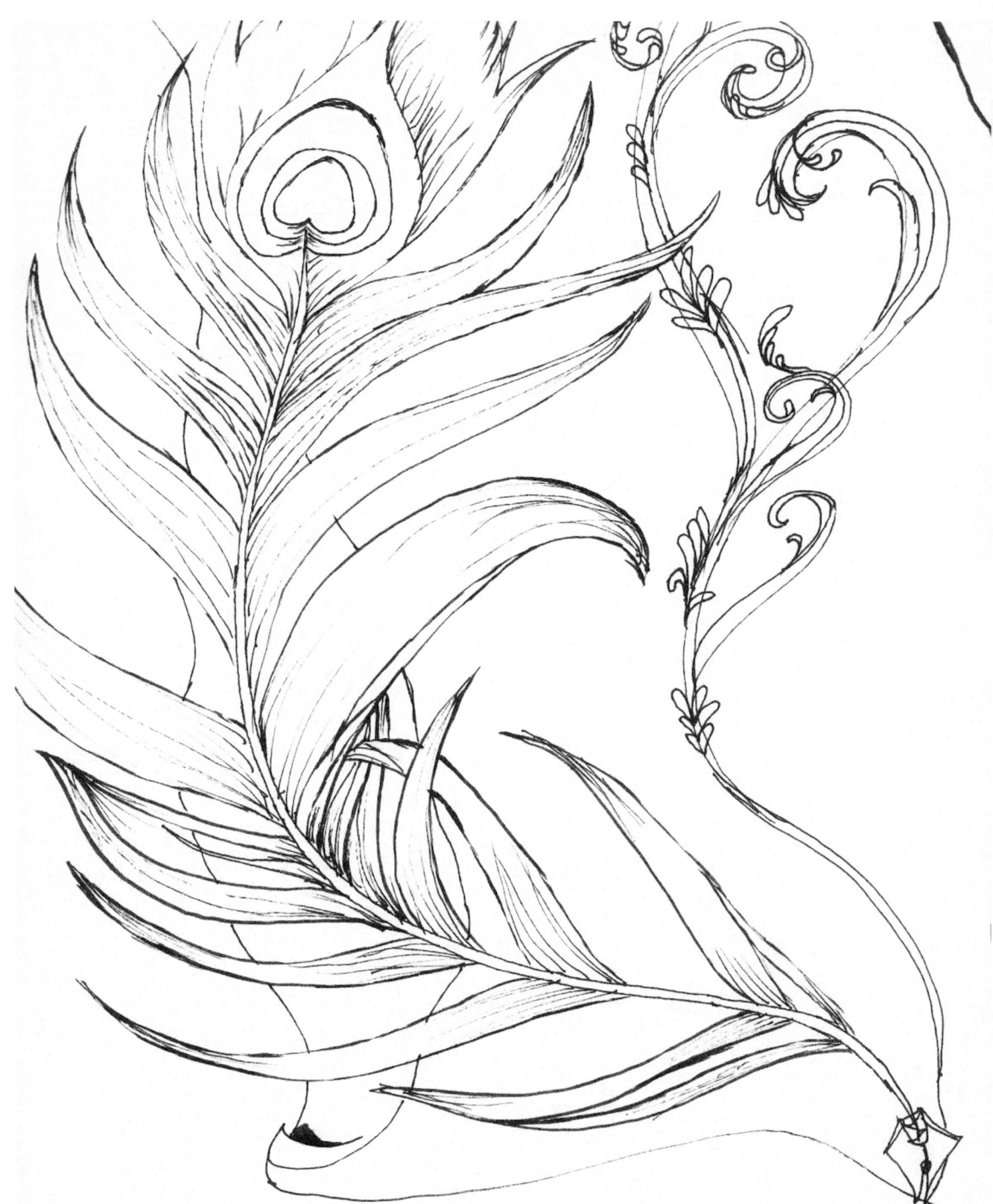

15

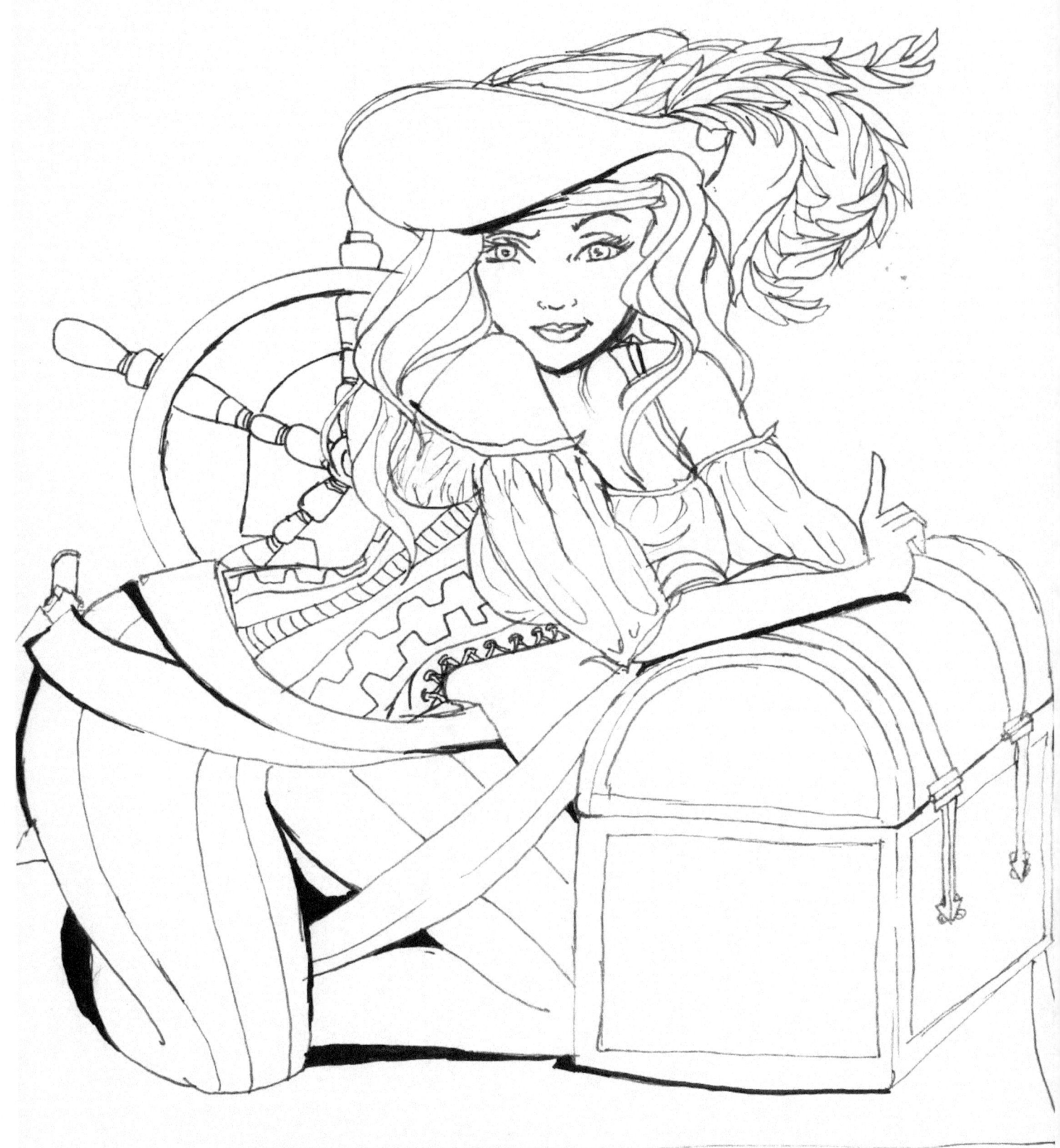

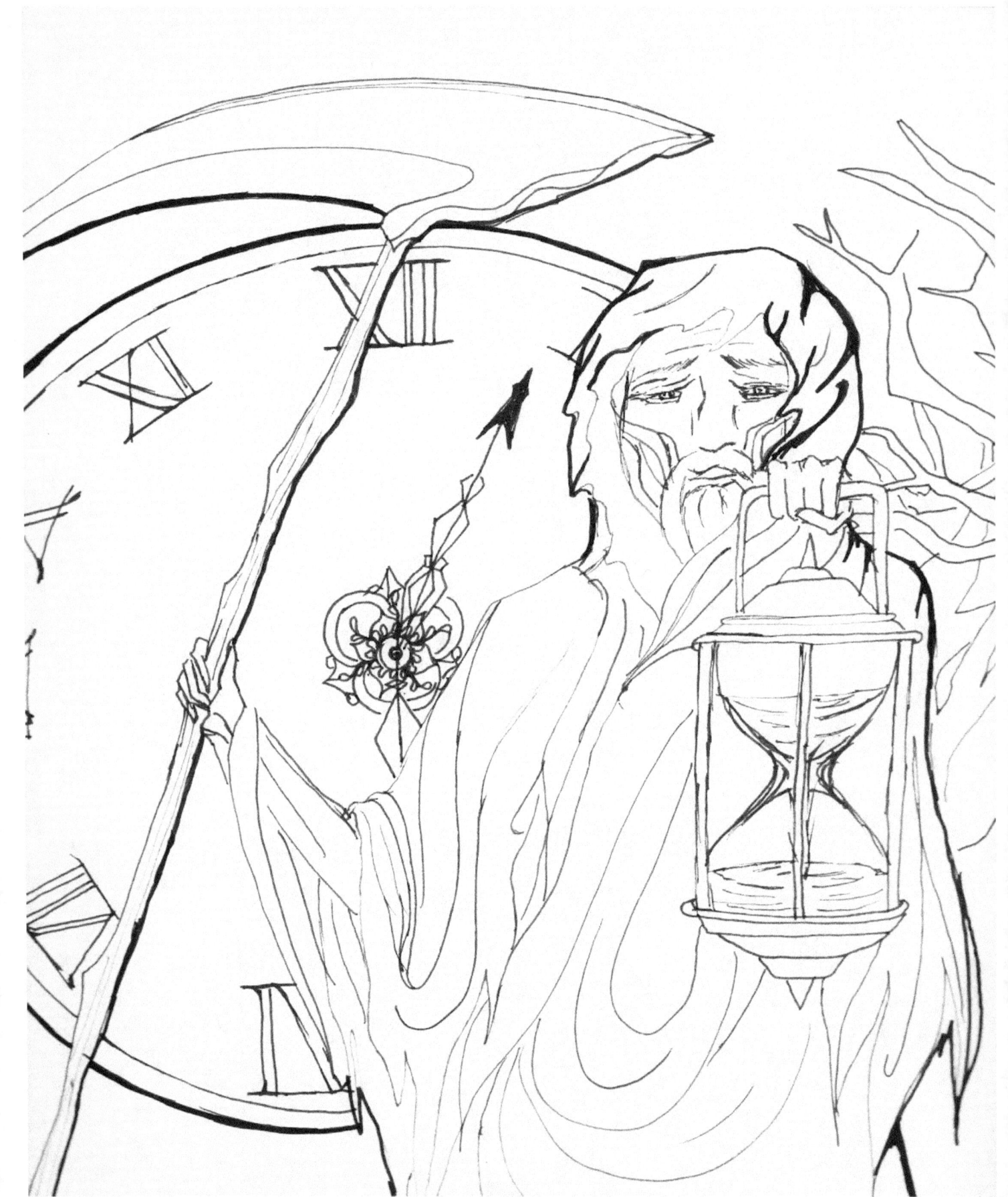

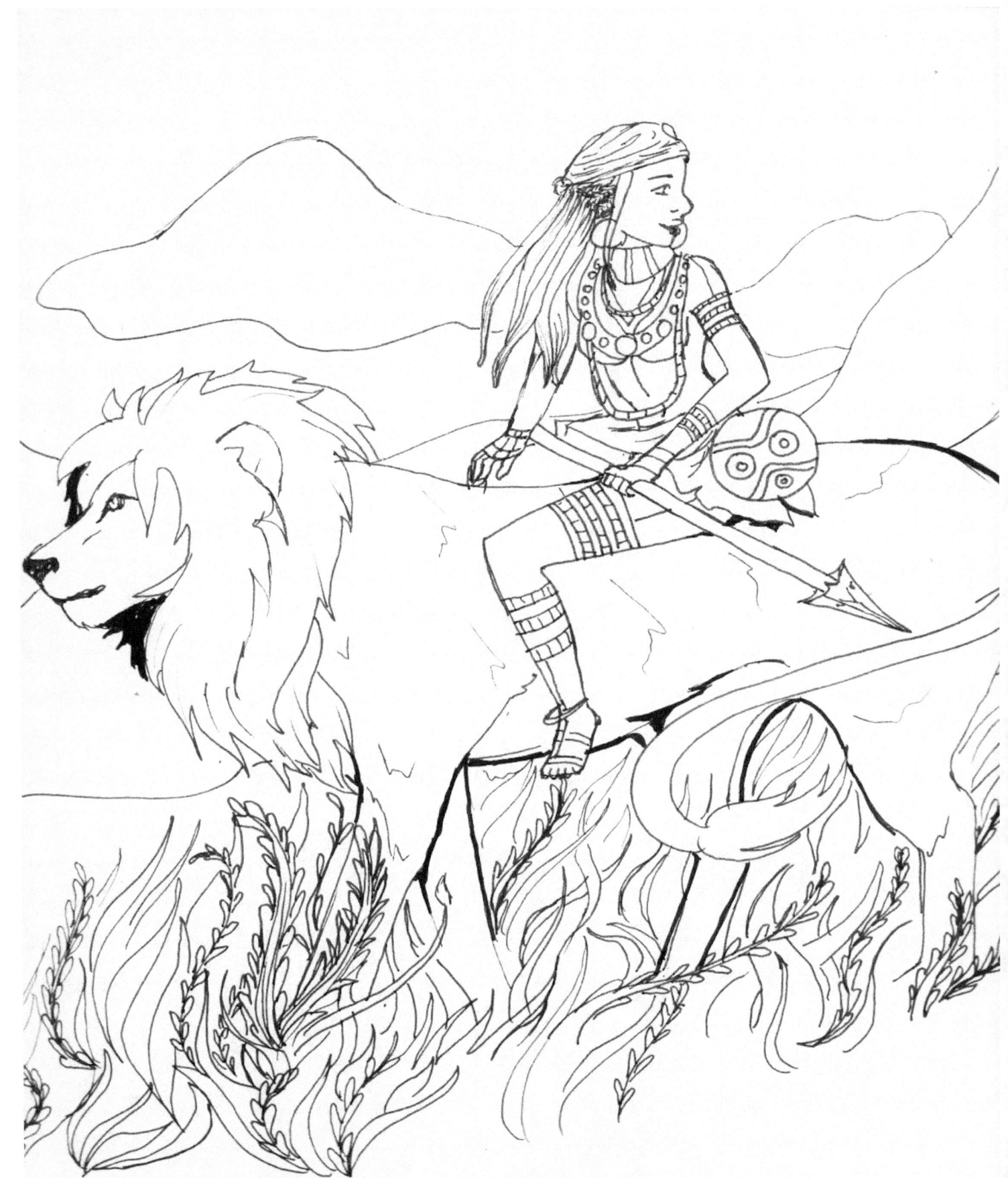

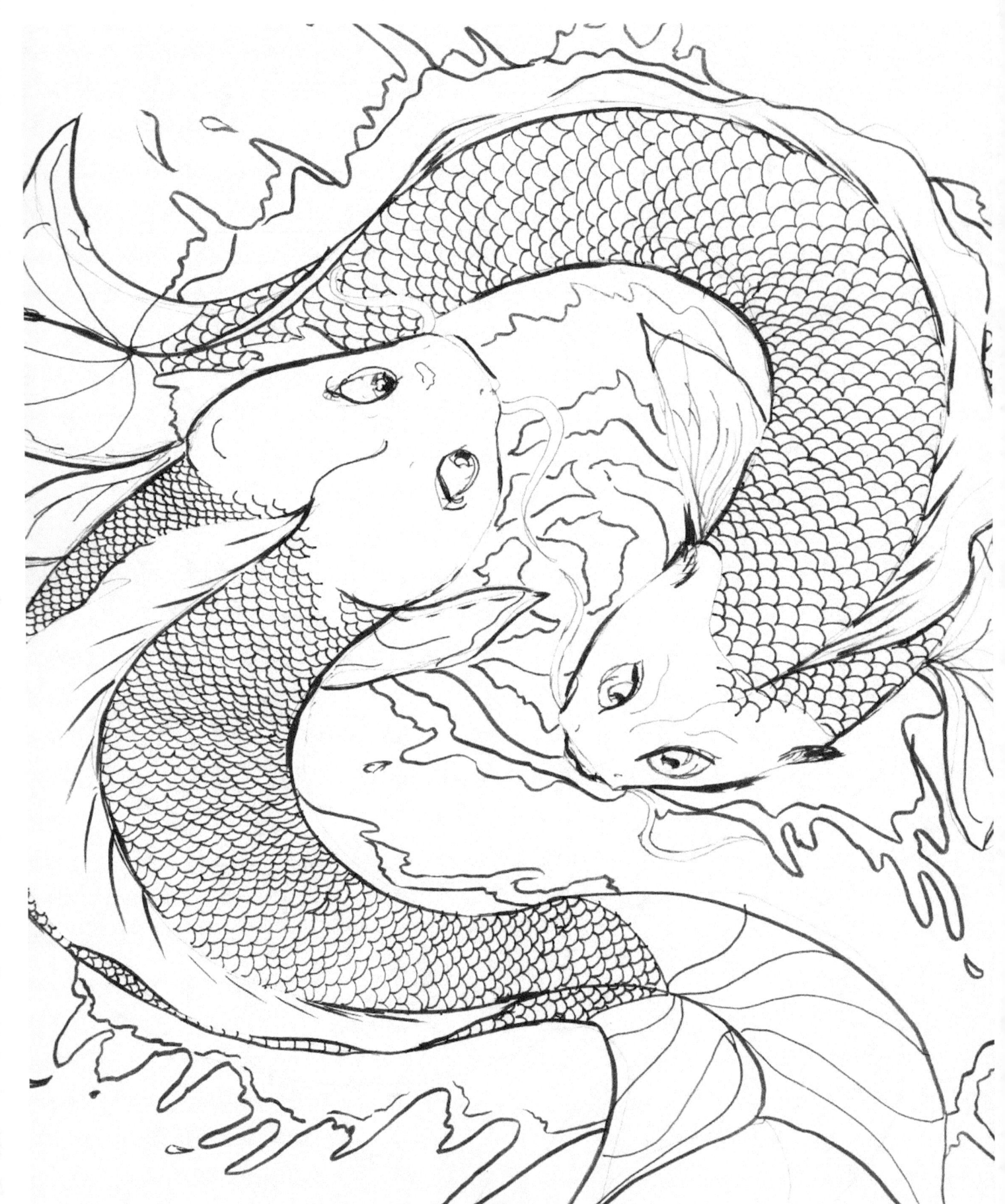

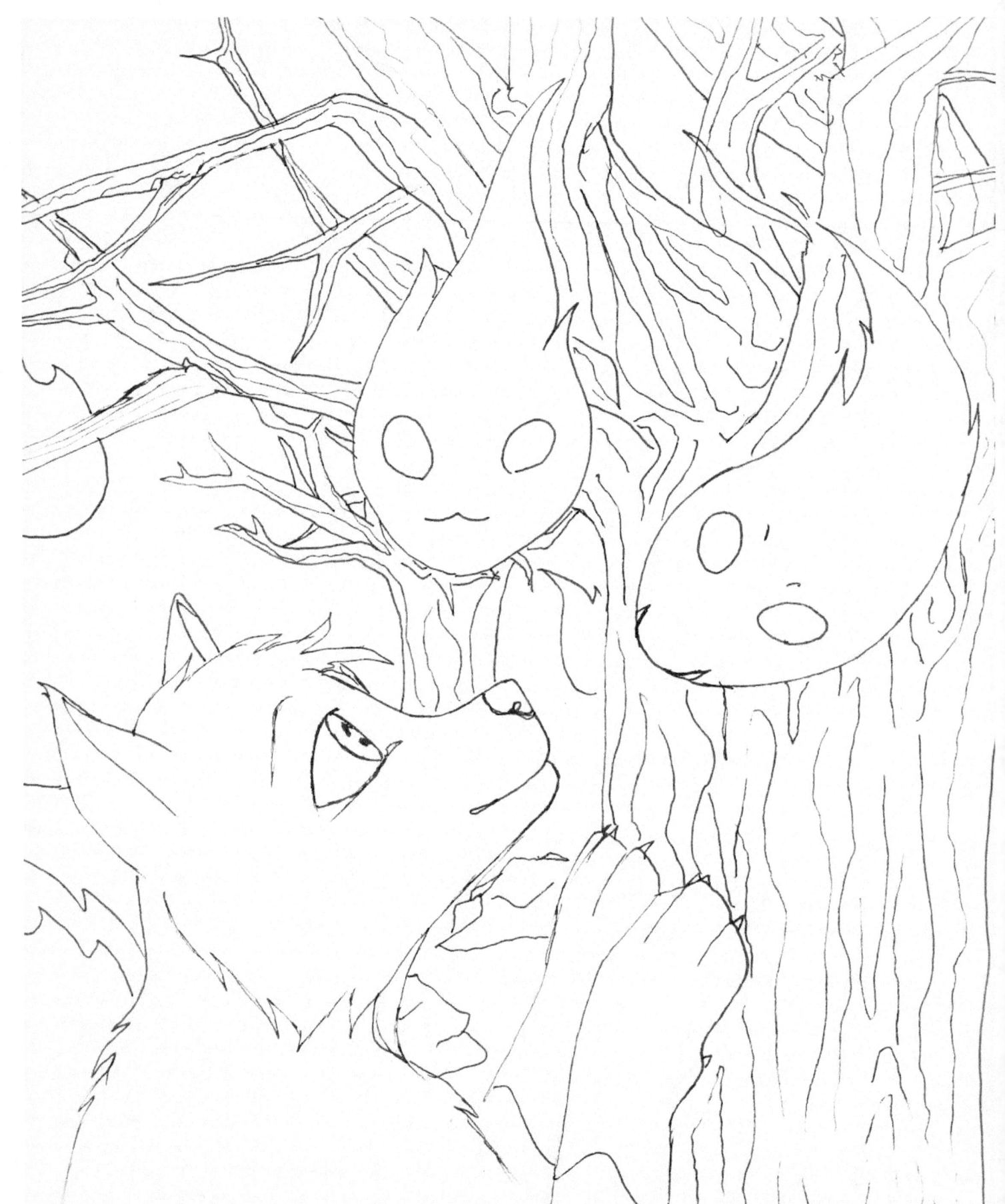

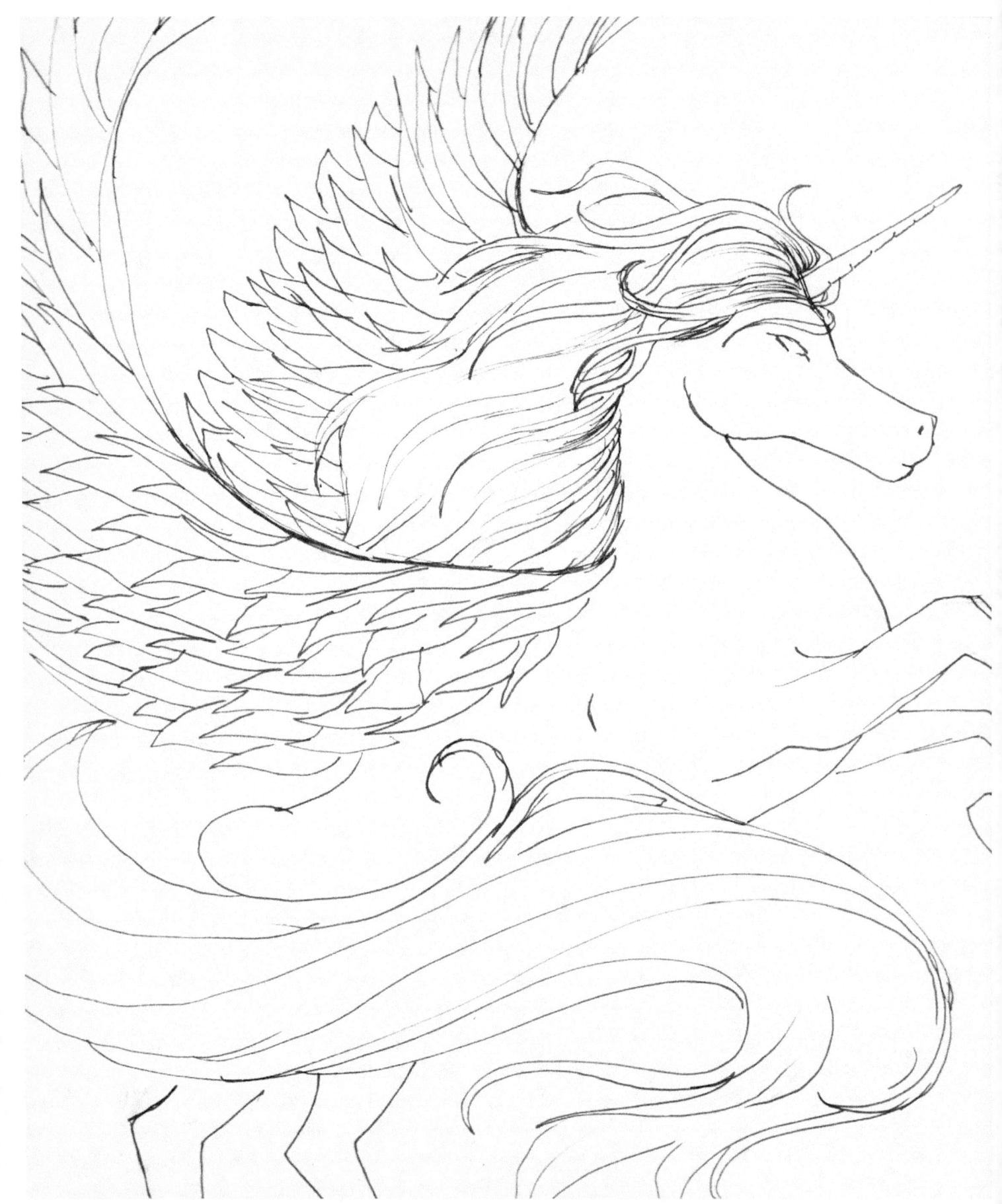

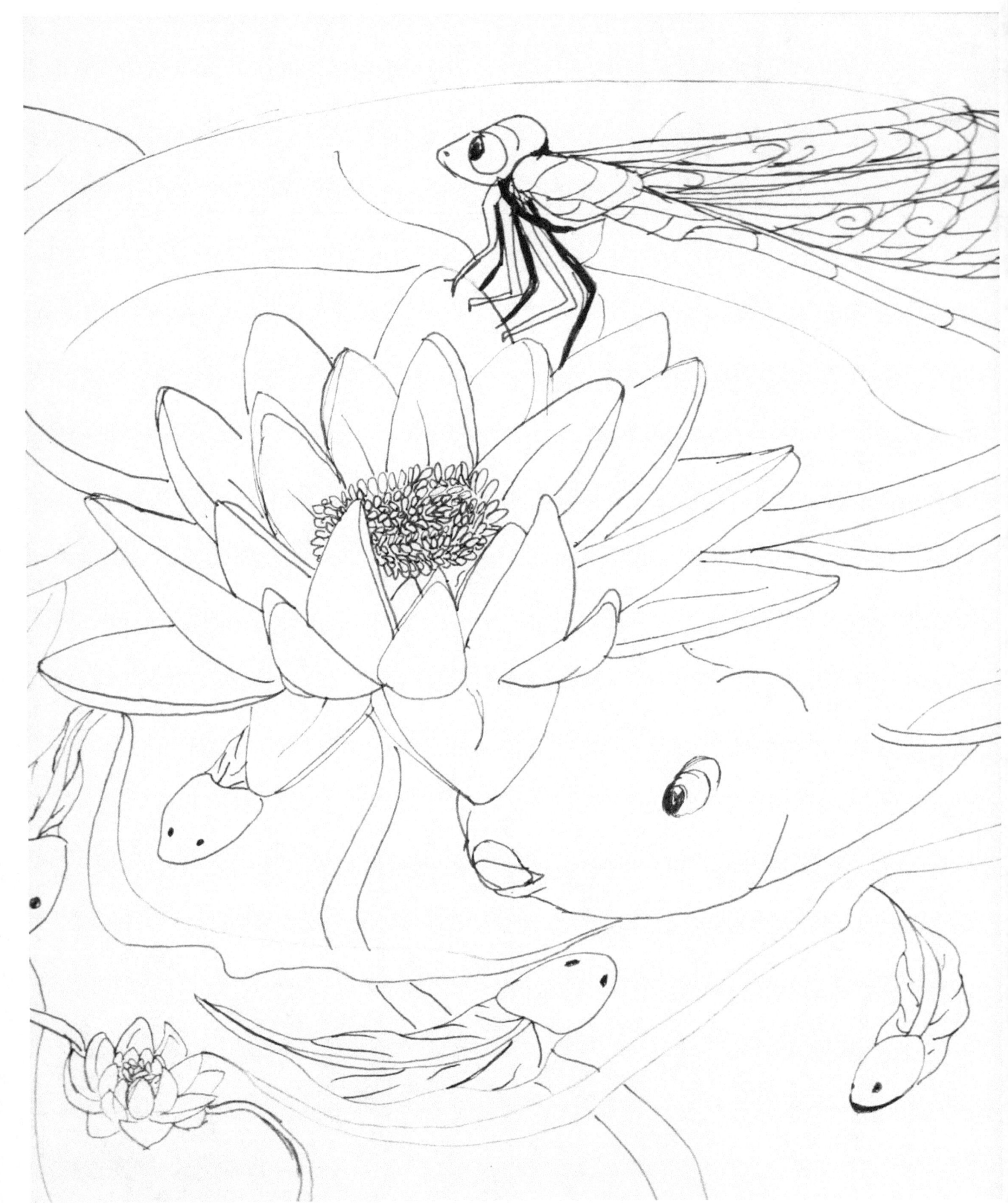

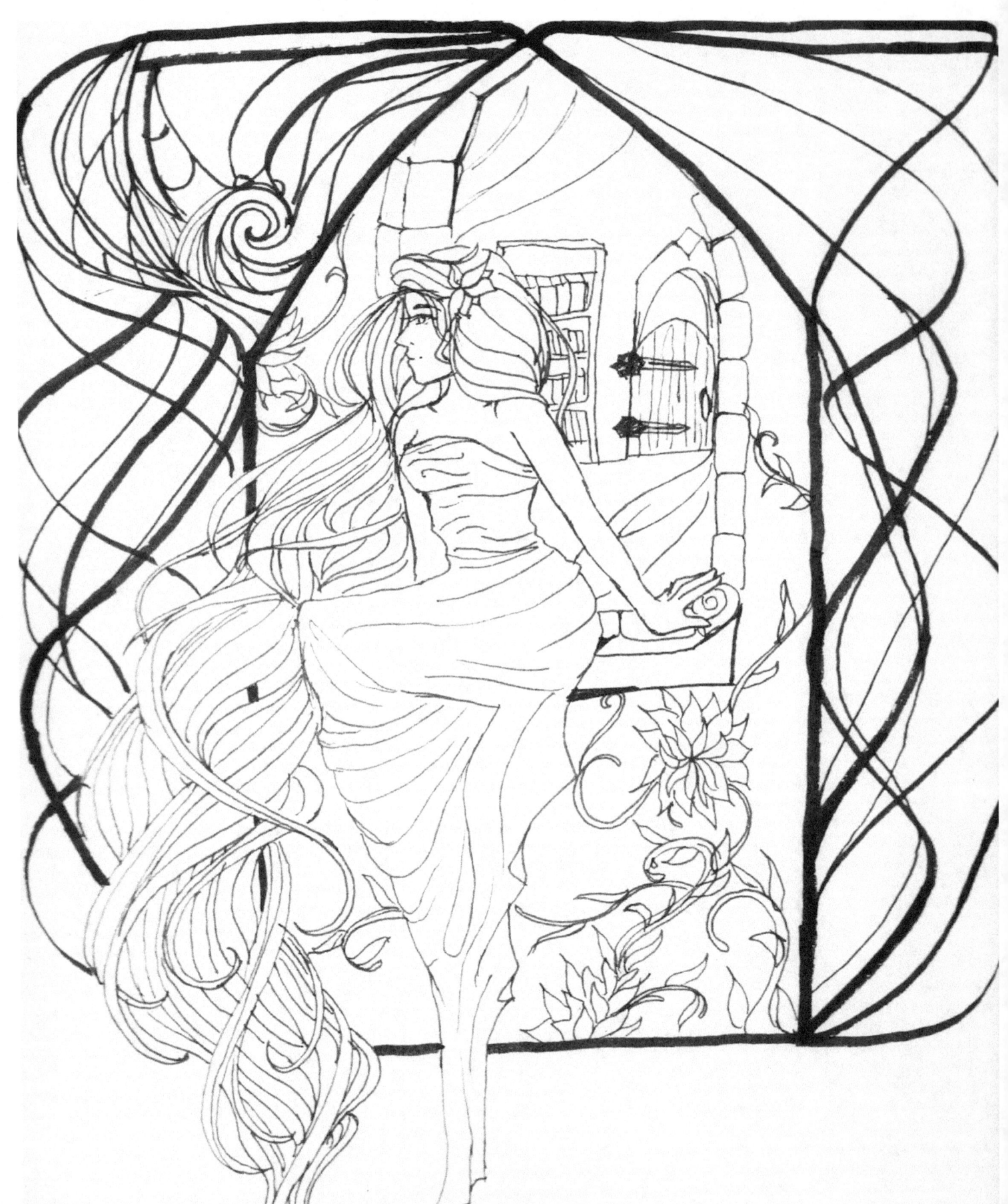

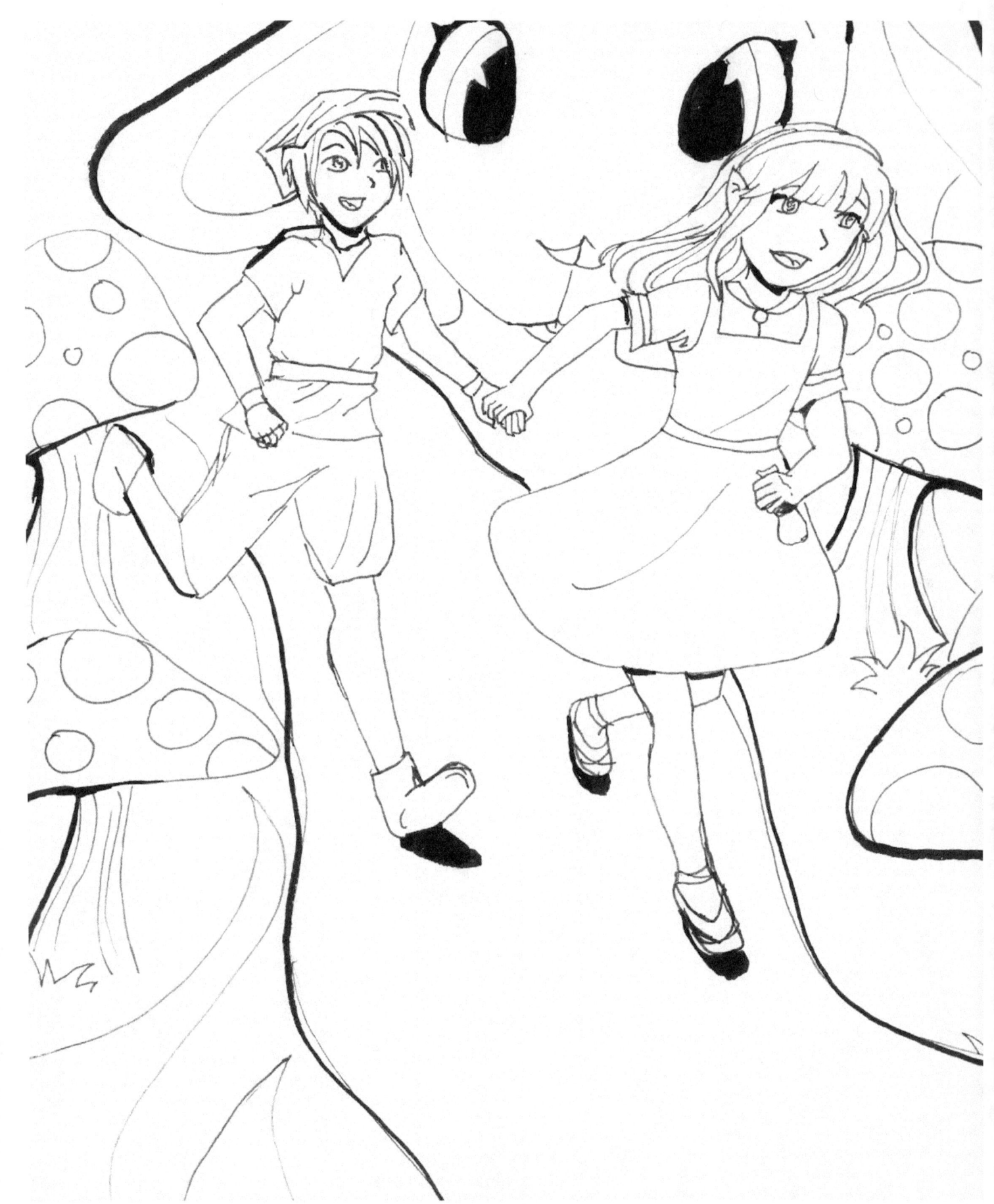

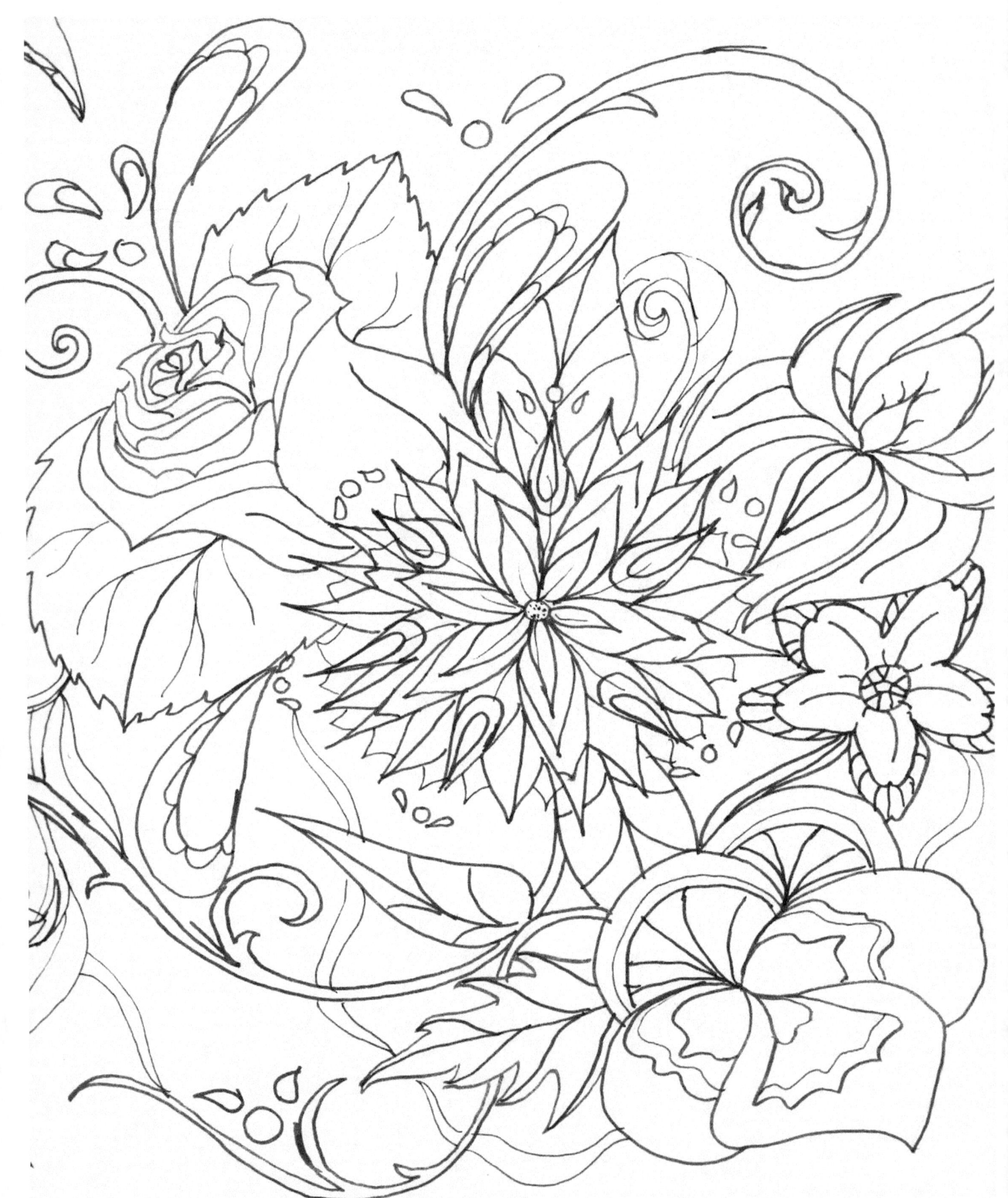

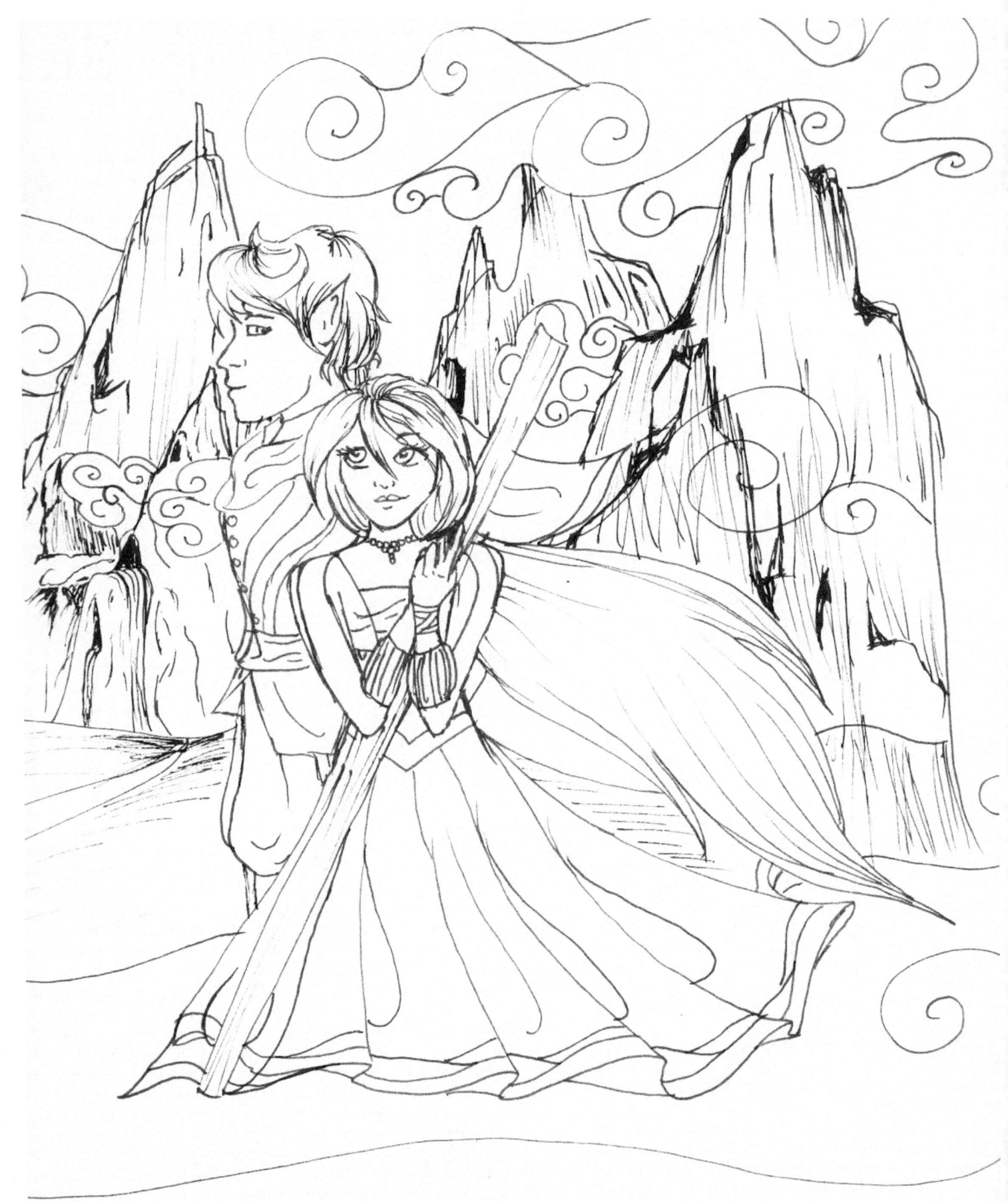

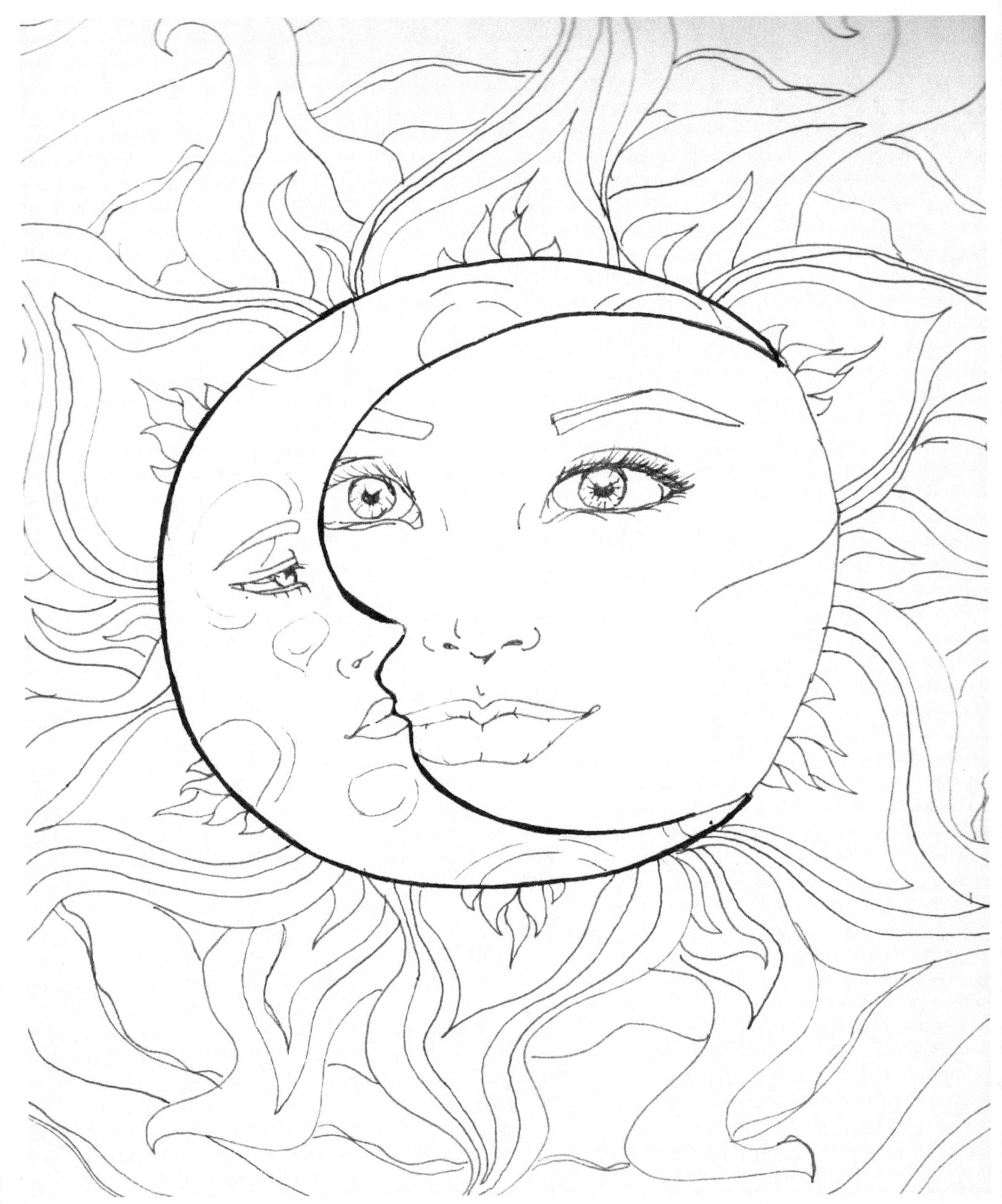

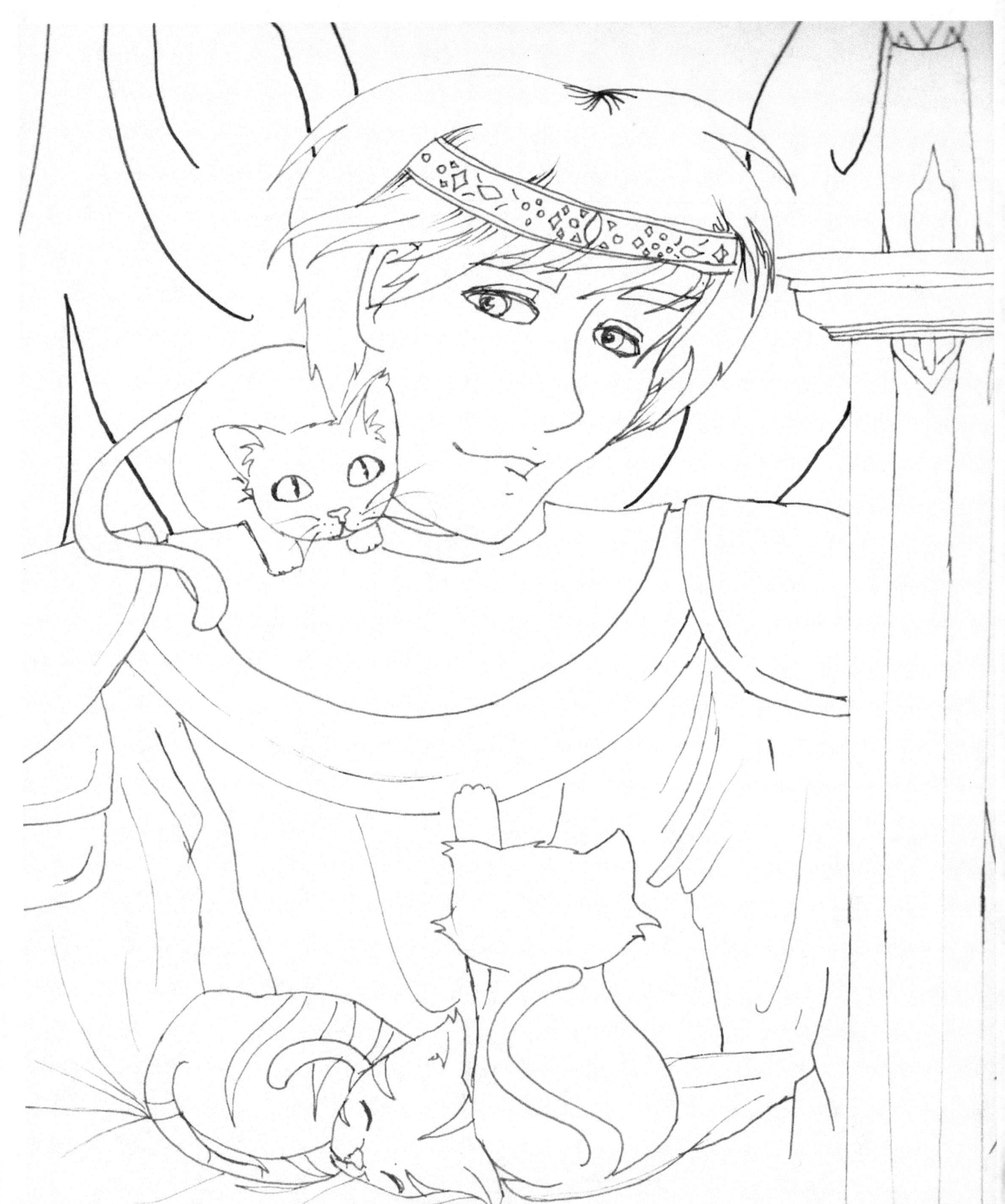

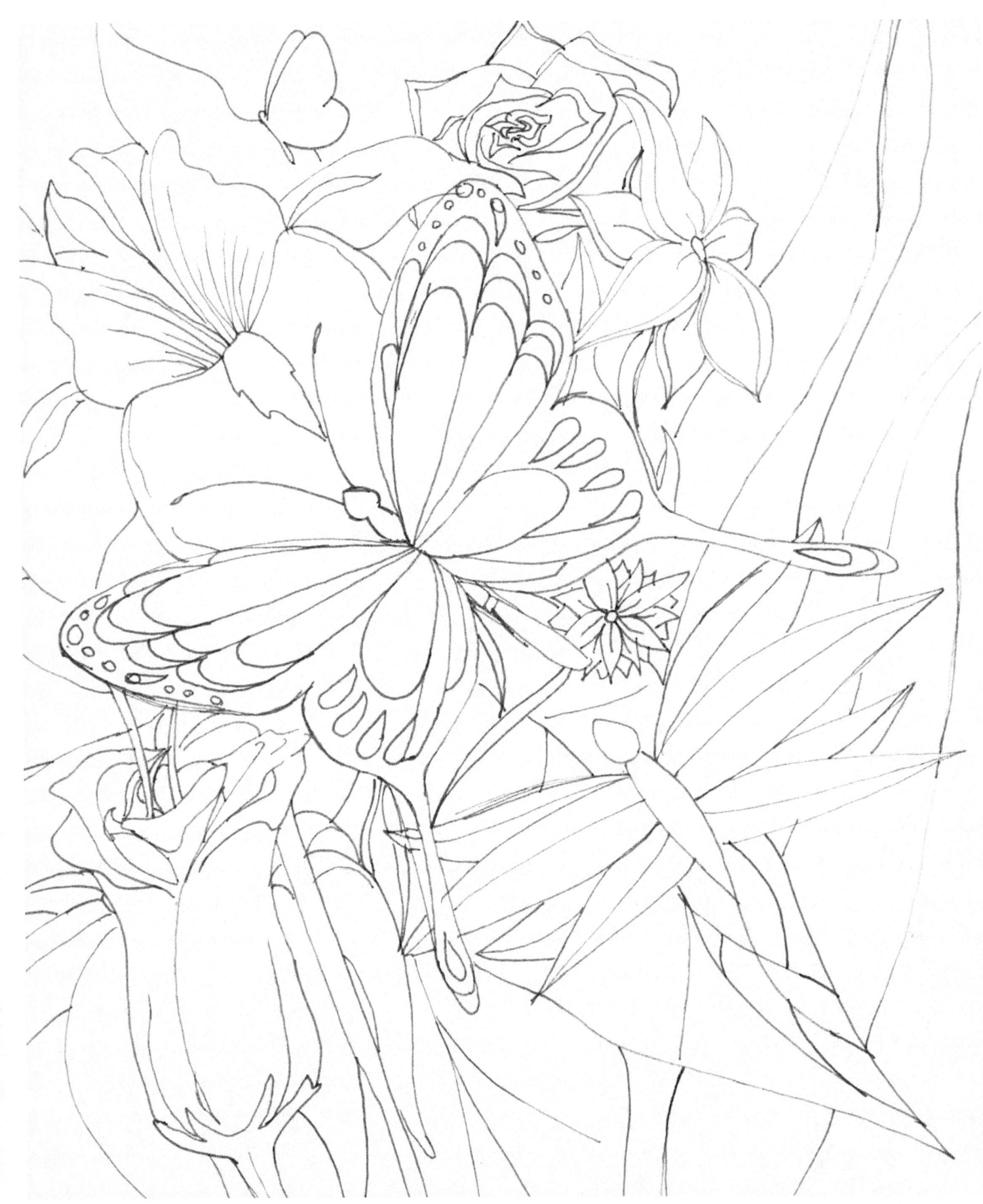

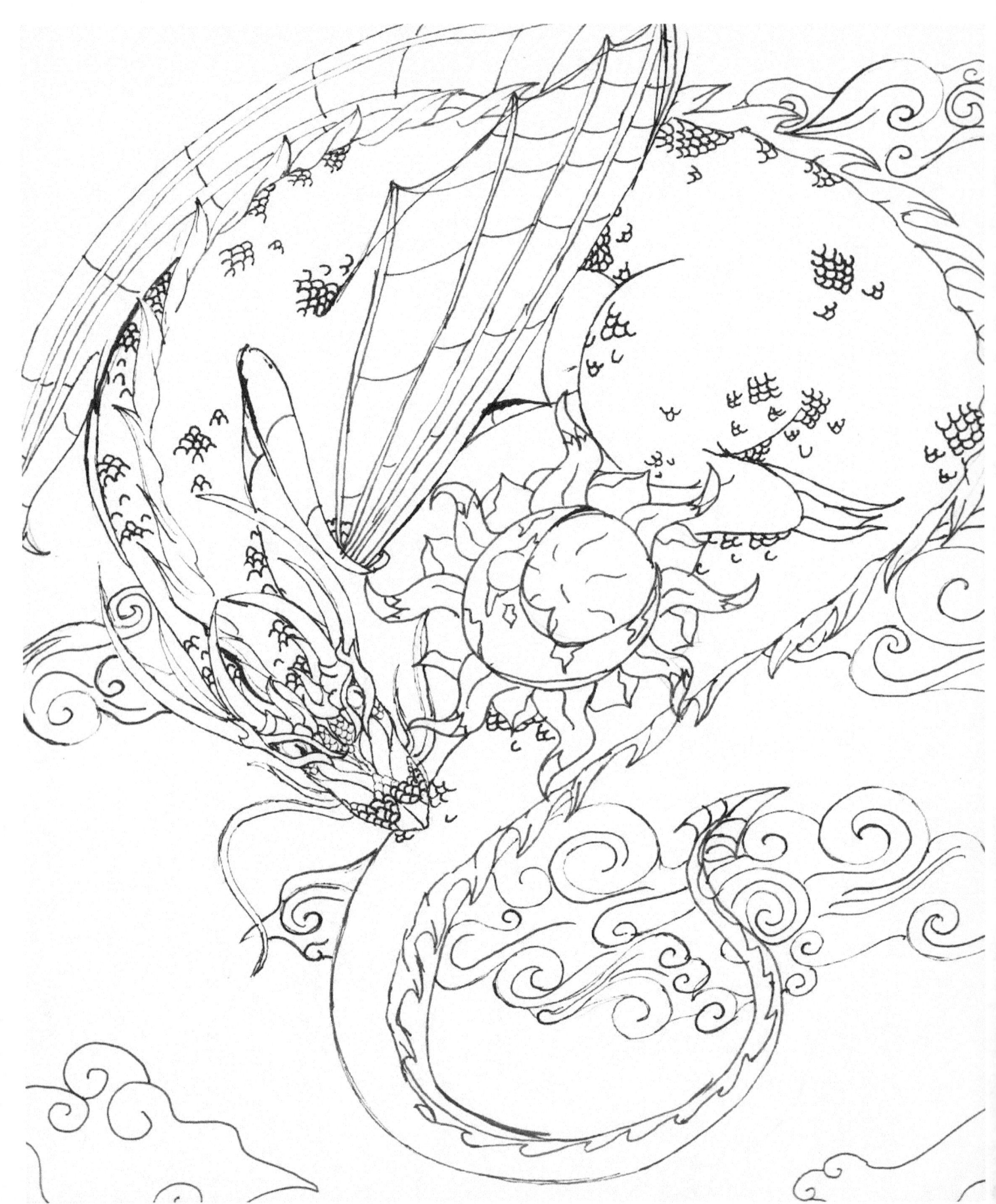

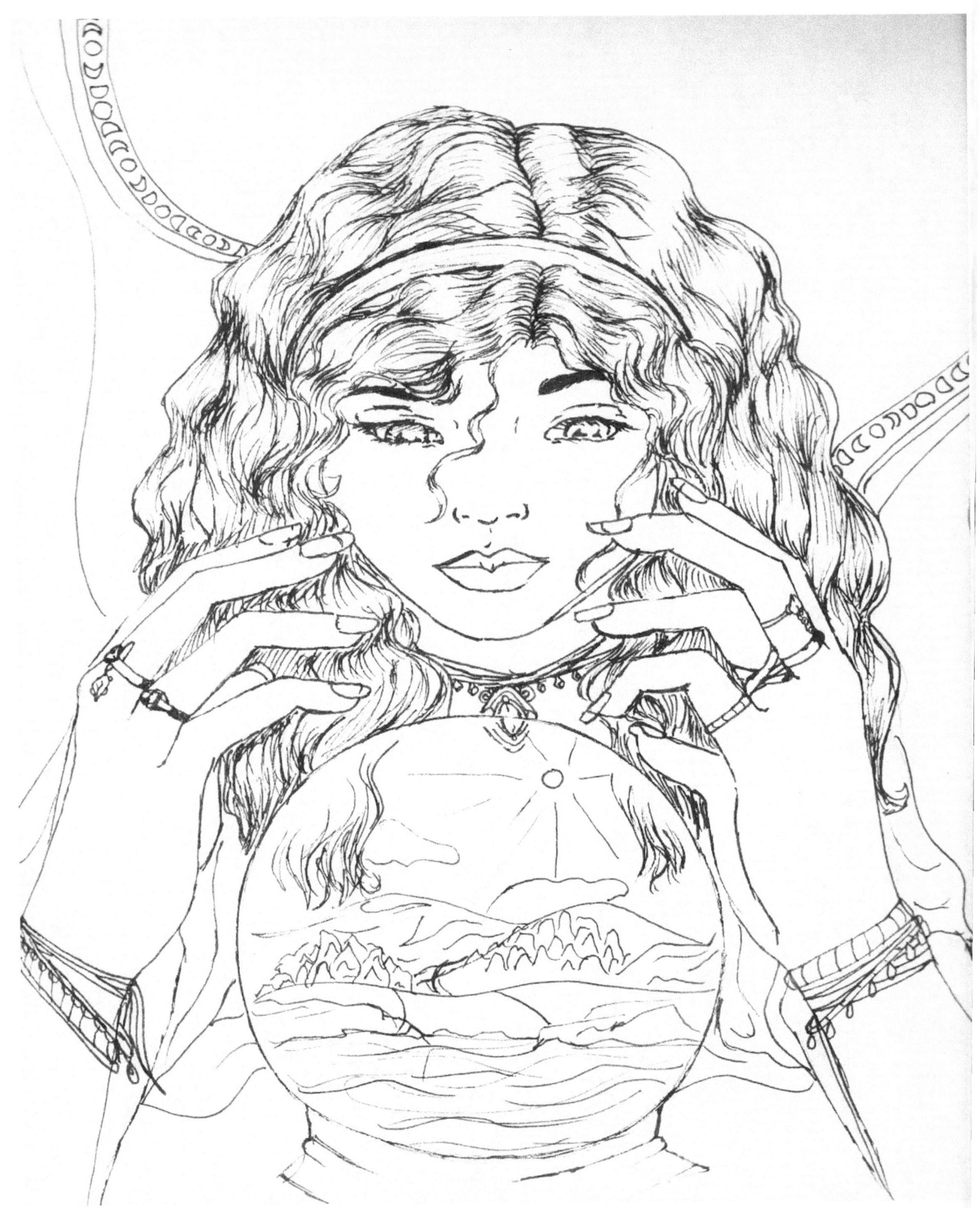

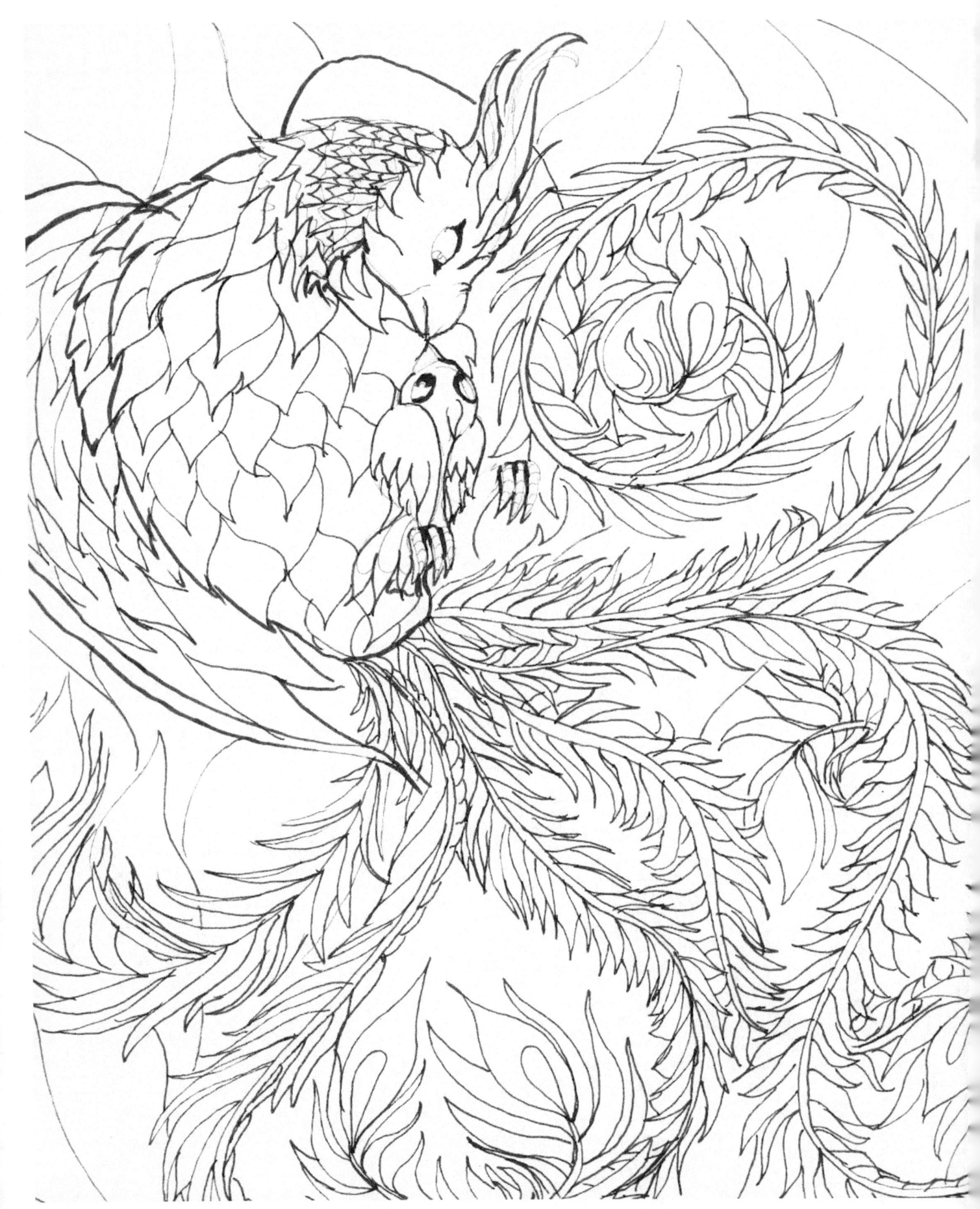